THE BOOK OF MONOLOGUES AND REVELATIONS

THE BOOK OF MONOLOGUES AND REVELATIONS

✦

ORIGINAL CONTEMPORARY
DRAMATIC
AND COMEDIC PERFORMANCE
MONOLOGUES
FOR ACTORS *AND* AUDIENCES

WITH TIPS AND SUGGESTIONS ON HOW TO AUDITION EFFECTIVELY AND GET CAST.

Nick C. Koroyanis

iUniverse, Inc.
New York Lincoln Shanghai

THE BOOK OF MONOLOGUES AND REVELATIONS
ORIGINAL CONTEMPORARY DRAMATIC AND COMEDIC PERFORMANCE MONOLOGUES FOR ACTORS *AND* AUDIENCES

Copyright © 2007 by Nick C. Koroyanis

All rights reserved. No part of this book may be used or reproduced by any means, graphic, electronic, or mechanical, including photocopying, recording, taping or by any information storage retrieval system without the written permission of the publisher except in the case of brief quotations embodied in critical articles and reviews.

iUniverse books may be ordered through booksellers or by contacting:

iUniverse
2021 Pine Lake Road, Suite 100
Lincoln, NE 68512
www.iuniverse.com
1-800-Authors (1-800-288-4677)

Because of the dynamic nature of the Internet, any Web addresses or links contained in this book may have changed since publication and may no longer be valid.

The views expressed in this work are solely those of the author and do not necessarily reflect the views of the publisher, and the publisher hereby disclaims any responsibility for them.

Copyright 2007 Library of Congress
Registration Number PAu3-107-216

ISBN: 978-0-595-46985-7 (pbk)
ISBN: 978-0-595-91269-8 (ebk)

Printed in the United States of America

This book is dedicated to my teachers, mentors, colleagues, family, friends and all of its readers.

Nick C. Koroyanis

Contents

Foreword.. ix

Monologues... 1

Choosing a Monologue......................................36

Headshots...38

Preparing a Monologue.....................................39

Getting a call to Audition................................42

Auditioning...44

Creating Opportunity......................................46

Epilogue..47

FOREWORD

The primary purpose in sharing this original material is to give actors and performers audition monologue choices and suggestions on how to audition effectively. It is also my hope that a general audience finds this book entertaining and insightful.

I tried to keep these monologues as short as possible without sacrificing meaning and context. Where possible, I divided some of the lengthier monologues into sub-monologues by repeating some of the information to make them autonomous for an audition performance.

I hope that you find these monologues inspiring, and rehearsing them a satisfying process. If you are in need of clarification, or suggestions on how to approach any of these monologues, please feel comfortable to e-mail me at Monologuesandrevelations@Yahoo.com. Provide me with some background on the type of actor that you are, and I will respond with my suggestions. Nothing makes me happier than when friends and colleagues reach their artistic dreams and aspirations.

Nick C. Koroyanis

MONOLOGUES

(To plan; to anticipate; to hope)

It would be fun to meet someone fun, to meet for a date! I screw up just thinking about meeting and dating, but I'm determined to get it right! I look for dating opportunities everywhere I go! The other day, I waited fifty minutes for the bus! Mad as hell, I got on last, to let the driver have it. I looked at him and said; I've waited fifty minutes for you! "I'm sorry, I'm here," he said and smiled. He was sincere, and handsome. It's not your fault, I said, and took one of those seats for the handicapped—the dateless ones! I couldn't take my eyes off of him and he knew it. He'd turn and smile every now and then, and I smiled right back! I was so proud of me! I even asked him if this was his regular route, and he said yes! There is a chance; I created opportunity! If he remembers me next time, I will give him this coupon I have for a free burrito with no expiration date, and my card. I carry some with my last name crossed out. I think it's sexy!

(To justify; to accept)

I wasn't planning on prostituting myself and sure as hell, don't remember ever saying; when I grow up, I want to be a prostitute. It happened! There's always been someone willing to pay for intimacy. I learned on easy money! At 16, I *knew* I was smart, to not have to work for minimum wage at a fast food joint! At 25, I'm just not good at holding a job steady! Stepping out, selling some of me is the back up plan! With all these guys looking for a quick fix, it's a plan that works! I'm my own business, my own temp agency worker, my own ATM! When I'm in between career opportunities, I stroll down the places all kind of men go out looking. Friendly and assertive I approach with a how's it going? Is there anything I can help you with! The rest is easy!

(To shock; to share professional secrets)

1984! Tina Turner's "Private Dancer" and I were a big hit that year. It was my theme song! I danced to it provoking pure guilt mixed with pleasure, my technique was exquisite. All I needed was a chair, a pole, a solid dance floor, stiletto heels and most definitely a spot light. I was born to be an Exotic Dancer. I made my audience strip itself of its dignity and morality. I listened to the primal voice within and obeyed a force of nature. When the goddess of seduction appeared no one resisted temptation! You didn't have to get with me to sin. Oh, no! I didn't turn tricks like some girls did, so they could make the money to feed their boyfriends. I made plenty dancing. I was an artist, not a whore looking for a window display to prostitute myself! I added a little class to every place I worked! I was different. Those were the days!

(To entice; to intrigue; to exaggerate)

I headlined every major exotic club in the world. New York to L.A. to Vegas; Paris to Tokyo, too many to mention! I was the full figured beauty who surpassed expectations in arousing men and women. A novelty attraction in a skinny world of flesh, in lace and silk I lingered to middle-eastern music like a snake in the Garden of Eden! Seducing, tempting, and calculating with every twist and turn, I captured the energy of the entire place. A true performer would understand that! I took the stage, the pit, the orchestra, the balconies, and forced everyone to gasp in disbelief, that the road to heaven is curved like a slice of cool watermelon in the desert. I retired at the zenith of my career, and came home to this overgrown village of three million to teach all kind of women the ways one's body can mystify itself, and others. If a woman can look in the mirror and arouse herself, there is no straight man, who will not cut and serve his balls on a gold platter to have her! That's how you marry a millionaire!

(To teach; to inspire; to encourage; to lead the way)

Alright, listen up! Don't follow the music, become the music. Slowly turn your hips in full circle from right to left, 360 degrees; then left to right another 360 degrees. Belly dancing is exotic only when it suggests temptation. Keep the stakes high. Say the man you want is standing at the gates of heaven, which are about to open; great belly dancing can make him turn around, forget about heaven and follow you to hell if that's where you want to go! So, turn your hips around, and around, and around. See yourself as a weeping willow with its branches hanging, softly embracing and dancing with the breeze. Your upper body is a bush tempting exotic birds to nest in its foliage, and your lower body rooted in soil full of nutrients. You can take someone to mystical places only if you can go there yourself. Good! That's very good. Now, move your fingers like a Hindu Indian goddess of destruction inviting the man she's singled out to the crater of her volcano.

Will she make it erupt? Will she sacrifice him? She hasn't decided, but it's totally up to her. Good job! Very good!

(To come to terms; to reminisce; to get a point across)

I was attracted to older men, and then I got old myself and quit being attracted period! I didn't master the dating rules but I played the game often, never with a guy my age. Older men in their late thirties, even forties were established, mature and very committed, elsewhere! It didn't bother me; weird enough, I found it sexy! Commitment is scary. With so many flowers in the garden of life, why settle for one rose, if there is a lily nearby! So, I learned to be the other woman, welcomed gifts—tokens of appreciation, nothing extravagant like diamonds; a sweater, a gold bracelet, sexy lingerie, just enough to keep my attention and it worked! Regrets? Not really! What else could have happened that didn't already happen? It's not like I turned down the love of my life because he was young, rich and handsome! I was naive, even stupid, but in retrospect I learned early on that maybe one person isn't enough to last a life-time. Committed people stray to find excitement, and go home feeling better about misery. No one is forever someone else's!

(To entertain; to reveal; to accept)

I was mesmerized by all the whacked out people who think out loud in the subway, the buses, and the streets. I tried to remember every word, and if I could afford to miss my stop, I did; just in case a profound revelation would escape the lips, I thought God borrowed to speak in twisted tongues; a message that'd change my life. It didn't happen! No higher intelligence than mine showcased itself through a person drowned in emotional and intellectual chaos. I've gotten more answers from a pair of eyes filled with warmth and serenity overwhelming me with a sense of acceptance, than any guru, or self-help book on meditation! Perhaps, answers find us when we realize questions shouldn't be as complex, and that the essence of life is to remain beyond my grasp forever intangible!

I can't tell if some messed up people are on drugs, or need drugs! What they talk about to imaginary friends is mind boggling. The other night on the train, this man went on and on about hospitals, doctors and cancer treatment in great detail, in a killer monotone speech. This tube and that tube; this pill and the side effects of that procedure, and more tubes, more pills and I.V.s non-stop! He had to be crazy for some time, or went crazy when he got the hospital bill! I wanted to tell him to wrap it up, but didn't dare; he was so into it, having a great time with all of this newfound knowledge, which could have spared my ears and brain! I wonder if cancer hadn't been the most interesting thing that happened in his life; if it wasn't a *miracle* that gave him a measure of truth, a standard, a long awaited purpose to decide if fighting for life is worth it!

(To understand; to make sense)

Saints visit my dreams asking me to believe that Jesus was the son of God, who came to earth to save us! Jesus! A mystic, a scholar, a being torn and tormented by the spirit under the flesh! He mirrors the ultimate of human struggle, the martyrdom that comes in a quest to believe, yet satisfying to the mind! Jesus! A journey in reverse; divine spirit descending to experience humanity! How does the spirit of the divine manifest and balance itself in human nature? Is the impossible and the possible the same depending on how you look at each? Jesus! What was he thinking? If someone came today proclaiming to be the son of God, what would you think? Drugs!

(To witness a revelation; to experience intercession)

I believe in the modern saints of my time; Saint Therese of Lisieux, the little flower; the Blessed Mother Teresa! I've seen photographs, read interviews; they are part of a contemporary world; a consciousness I can understand, even relate. A saint must have stirred my attention at the horizon of the lake the moment a rainbow cut through the vastness of the water like a sword shooting up in the sky piercing the clouds. A rainbow so wide, each color defined, vividly diffused on both sides giving way to the color next to it. That was the moment I knew; God is here all around; in the miracle of nature that feeds our imagination and sustains our bodies. And for the first time God was real; an entity, a force of energy presenting itself before my eyes. That's when I knew that we are in God and in heaven right here on earth; heaven we flip into hell with every unkind act of war to another and ourselves! I taste this heaven all around, and can't get enough of it!

(To motivate; to inspire; to report; to document)

He is calling on me to awaken the little God within to help and make a difference. How? Choose to be different! How? Fight your indifference; awaken the life force resting in Oblivion Country! It's not that simple, I said. It isn't difficult, he answered. Profound! So, I attended a free BYOB lecture God was hosting by the river. Only God could transform the intellectual to spiritual to emotional with such ease and grace. He didn't talk about anything new, starting his speech with a little guilt trip on how we are responsible, not him, for people suffering in far away places. If you have a lot here, take the overflow where it can do some good. You don't have to be God to think like that! Trade the luxury cruise for a free ticket on a cargo ship, and help to unload it at a distant forgotten country that CNN has ignored. Unload food, medicine, supplies, and hope! Love is a byproduct of actions designed to serving the inherent goodness in you. You are capable; it is doable and real. Aren't I real, he asked! I am an active flow of energy whose only side effect is peace, he said. Do something to restore the spirit of another; mend someone's heart, but first feed the body for Christ's sake! Privilege is a blessing you share, and as you pass it on, it multiplies. Look for those in need. Surprise! They're closer than you think. Approach! Caution! Take the time and do some good. Give a blessing, a word of encouragement, a pound of rice; perform an ordinary miracle of kindness. Start and keep *going, and going and going*, and I will always keep your batteries charged. Hell, I might bring the lottery your way for your efforts, he said, and bid us goodnight! He had another lecture to give. I stood there watching him board "Air Force 1" and didn't know what to make of it!

(To solve a riddle)

My pastor is bright and inspiring; I love him! Last Sunday he said, we are a part of God by definition, but didn't define the definition! Neither we, nor God are the unknown X in his equation, he said. I'm glad he knows the equation of God to solve it, because equations and I are completely unrelated! I didn't want him to think I'm stupid and I didn't ask, but it's been bugging me to find the answer. Maybe he meant that we are God's creation sharing in his ability to create life anew with a twist of the devil to destroy it. Or, could it be that because we can communicate with God, we can express and imitate him? I don't know! Maybe it was just a fancy line, a metaphor, an intrigue of sorts to keep us coming back to church, a feel good ploy to give more cash; or just a figure of speech that we are a part of God by definition. But then again, if God is love, and we are capable of love, can love be what he meant!

(To awaken; to react)

I'm so caught up with the business of life; I forget to look at the expressions of God all around me. I take quick looks at the bare trees, the snow resting on the ground, the vast lake embracing my city, but don't process the images, my viewing is superficial. It's pathetic that living and sharing this planet with God, we need to go on vacation to interact with the divine, and when we are at home we walk along side-by-side ignoring each other, looking at opposite directions! I am displacing happiness and postponing joy when I don't allow nature to affect me. I am capable of seeing, but with my brain racing, I have no time to look! Instead, I perform the mundane rituals of manmade habits, which have me go around in circles, only to get lucky to deviate from the circle with a new idea, which widens it to include more of us in this global economy of one land! Our ultimate destination of co-existence has everything to do with co-dependency, which we fight so very hard to avoid!

(To wish; to visualize one's death)

If death comes in my sleep, I will be the happiest dead person in the world. Crazy, but isn't sleep a death like break from living? Eight, seven, six hours when nothing really matters, no anxieties, no worries, no bills, no love affairs gone bad, no right, or wrong! If I die in my sleep, there'd be nothing I would know to miss. Of course, I hope the place was clean with no racy magazines on the night stand! It'd be embarrassing if I forgot some version of the 'young and the restless' in the DVD player, but I suppose I can live with that, being dead and all! I wish for an instant death, nothing prolonged! I don't want to see the angel coming! What am I going to say? Excuse me, I'm a little too busy here trying to stay alive, can we re-schedule? I'm not brave, but I don't want to be weak and torn in a battle I can't win! I don't want to know what lies ahead, and certainly don't want anyone coming back from the dead to tell me!

(To partake; to join; to revel)

Love transcends all being and becomes the energy of God. It is God I see when I walk by the lake; its depth and magnitude assure me it must be! The horizon's ever changing with clouds forming as if the water is exhaling a breath of amazing grace. This must be the house of God; maybe a summer home, for the Pacific Ocean is better suited for his primary residence. I can see God snoozing, stretching, and resting on this giant water mattress watching the show of creation in the sky—his own high definition screen; a mirror to take pleasure in himself with oyster and shrimp at arm's length to snack on! And all of the clouds, curtains and valances for privacy when he's not in the mood for a public appearance! What must I seem like in the eyes of God, but a toy like G.I. Joe playing in the sand! It's in this company I find the energy of my spirit, and I'm at peace when I experience this force travel through me in undefeated battles of movement and rebirth.

(To free; to sever ties; to take responsibility; to obsess)

You were a lie and a cheat; I know you didn't plan it, but I believed your lies and took the blame, mine and yours; I held on and dwelled in it for years! Holding on to us suffocated my spirit! Time went on and I followed. I lived to re-live and got spent trying to understand what was as I re-examined our past instead of pushing me forward to invest in the future. Erasing and excluding you from my present was impossible. You were the love of my life. I thought I was yours, too! It's obvious to me now that one can be another's love for a fraction of life; not a life-time, and I'm okay with that as I re-claim the spirit I let go; save what's left; replenish and smile at it again, I am!

(To despise; to envy; to come clean)

My best friend in high school got all the attention, and I got what was left over, if anything! She was a blond! Everybody loves blonds. King Kong loves blonds! Brunettes, have to take themselves to the gorillas, in the mist! Blonds! But, not every blond is popular. Men don't join the circus to meet and impress blonds from Wisconsin, Minnesota, and definitely not from Russia, or Poland! It's the California blonds! That's how deeply sexist the world of blonds is! In retrospect, I'm glad I wasn't trophy material; it motivated me to go to medical school and graduate with honors! I was beginning my six figure salary life, while Jennifer, my then best blond slut friend was ending her marriage *without* alimony! I'm not a blond, but can afford a blond attitude anytime I want. Life is good!

(To entertain)

Babies are cute, even children up to that awkward age of nine to fifteen when they are too insecure, and too obnoxious to be cute, and live to impress each other acting like the latest rapper and pop star! Then adulthood sets in, pretty babies are all grown up and the beautiful picture becomes a bad painting. The cute little nose is now a small eggplant; the ears protrude like alien space shuttles and the almond eyes don't make it beyond the sweet pea stage! An ongoing earthquake is altering the structure of our face like mid continental divides shifting and drifting apart. It only gets worse when you wake up in the morning and the first wrinkle has made its appearance on your forehead! Is it the Nile, or the Mississippi river? Before you know it, Africa and every major continent makes an entrance with no exit, and the texture of your skin succumbs to time with blemishes and spots like ecosystems of algae and the like! No one is safe from time; the only winner? Time!

All you need to meet a man is to strike a subtle, mindless, impertinent conversation. We live in a civilized society and spend millions of dollars on motivational speakers who give us the tools to overcome shyness, and replace passive with passion! Yes, you can volunteer, but why give up your only day off when you can snooze and spend some quality time with your cat? Volunteering does work, but if you're thirty, obviously don't volunteer at a nursing home; join a political campaign you can pretend to believe in! If you want to marry a man with Christian values, a church would be the place. But, if you want to try out the merchandise first, a church wouldn't be my first choice! It's hard to convince a man that the one night stand you had with him was your first one ever! Men are everywhere we are, looking as hard as we do! Get out there. Play the field and have fun doing it!

(To coach; to advice; to entertain)

Meeting a man requires some strategy; not that you want to be overly calculative perpetuating stereotypes—fancy words work, too! The grocery store! Why rush to buy and get out! A man should always be at the top of your grocery list. Scout the aisles; find a man you like and stalk him a bit; it wouldn't be illegal in a public place, and besides how can you stalk someone you don't even know, yet! Get in his way with your shopping cart! Say you are sorry, and modestly look down. He'll think you're shy and humble, and that's good! Men like women who they can corrupt! Look for wedding rings, clean and trim nails! Strike a conversation. Ask him where the cereal is! Plan the unplanned! Be on the look out. The cereal isn't going anywhere, but the men will if you don't follow and intercept them. Get creative and put your cart to use already!

(To guide step-by-step; to solve; to add; to entertain)

If you want to meet the cute man you run into at the grocery store, time yourself and get right before him, in the checkout line! It is perfectly acceptable to drop your car or home keys while you're looking for your wallet! As a gentleman he'll reach to get them for you, as you attempt to do the same! His groceries are on the belt right next to yours; you are next to each other by default. What he buys indicates if he's single—pizza, milk, bread, chips, beer, plenty of conversation starters. How is that beer? If what he buys is a nicely wrapped salad, a health drink, two bananas and a pint of premium ice cream, I'd be a little apprehensive, if you know what I mean! Start an insignificant conversation to break the ice. Pay for your items and get busy … waiting! The cashier is hopefully quick and has bagged his groceries while you are ready to head out. Revive the conversation even if it feels like CPR. Ask if he lives in the neighborhood! If he does, tell him you just moved there yourself. If he lives in another neighborhood, tell him that you're thinking about moving there, too! How is it? Are there any hot spots, events, things to do! Keep it casual, neutral, and non-threatening even as you are starring in "A little house on the prairie episode." If he doesn't play ball, he might be slow, or just didn't fancy you that night. It doesn't mean that he wouldn't ravage you the next time he sees you! Don't take it personally; just go shopping often!

(To confide; to share a secret)

I don't go to bars to meet men! Who wants to meet drunk grown up men who behave like boy scouts? I prefer to meet men on the bus. The more crowded the bus, the better! I choose a bus route that goes through a decent and established neighborhood. I go to the back of the bus to make room for others, but when I see someone cute I come forward to *see* if my stop is coming up! I'm sorry, I'm from out of town, I say, this bus is going downtown! I leave early for work, not because I need to get with London, or Tokyo, but just in case I need to get off before, or after my stop! Hi again, I say! Is east, that way? You know it is, but if west is where he's headed, then, west you must go! Where's a good place to lunch? Oh! I think I'm going to give it a try today! People in this city are, so *nice*! I should treat you to lunch for your kind help. I insist!

(To criticize; to vent; to bitch)

The laws of attraction never fail to appear. I'm sorry, but I hate when two older bigger women are talking and laughing it up in the bus for the entire forty-five minute ride at seven in the morning, I'm sorry! Worse when one of these two women is a man, better color coordinated and sitting more lady-like than the real woman! I'm sorry, but I just can't deal with any person carrying on the most boring conversation on their cell phone, at any time, but especially in the morning and late at night when nature quiets and I with it. How? Why would anyone participate in a boring ass conversation? Stupid me! There are *two* boring people! Talk, talk, talk without a sense of self and privacy! Why should big brother act any different? Spend sometime with you, it won't hurt! I hate when people, I'm sorry, I'm not trying to be negative, I love flowers, ice cream and pizza, but I hate when people pack their lunch in clear plastic bags. I'm sorry, but at seven in the morning, I don't need to see you're having a version of tuna casserole for lunch! Oh, and oversized back packs? Do you need all that at work! And those, who *don't* pick up after their dogs, eh? Don't get me started on the bubble gum!

(To point out the obvious; to stir up controversy; to expose the status quo; to unmask your fears; to act in a commercial food-drive).

This is a colorful city! The red line, the blue, the purple, the brown, the pink! Like our neighborhoods, black, white, Hispanic! Thank God for mass transit that brings us all together, forcing us to accept and tolerate each other; taking us to and from work; making us an integral part of the corporate team effort! I live in exile; I can enter the land of the free to work, and then cross the tracks to go home! The same house in my neighborhood costs $150,000.00 and in that, half a million? Oh! Our real estate taxes are cheaper to reflect the quality of our schools I bet! Do they raise taxes to justify exclusivity! Integration is a long way coming. We value and pursue individuality, so we can be different and better than each other. That's what's driving us apart, when in essence we're all meant to come together! I don't know if it is racism, or just the way human nature works!

(To give an interview; to answer questions; to articulate one's ideology; to derail).

My music is eclectic like humanity. I want to help every person become whole through my music. We are trees branching out gathering and processing information about each other in order to connect. One tree alone can't do it. It is the same with music. We need all types of music. Mine is just like you said, eclectic, or maybe I said that! When I compose, I look for the power sound has to impact the listener and diffuse itself in colors dressing one's soul with some inner understanding of this world. You don't have to be from Greenland to feel the common experience. Every one of us goes about exploring, and then come together to share this intoxicating magic of our planet, both good and bad, layers of magic within magic to its very core. That's how we create a better world. Our essence is to live in everlasting enchantment, and maintain order through music. I can't make it any clearer than this!

(To hold someone accountable; to blame; to break free)

It's been ten years Judy, and he pops up out of nowhere like he left my consciousness and snuck in the room below it. I guess that's why they call it the subconscious! What the hell! Where does the memory of him come up to disturb my early morning dreams in the dead of winter? Check it out! We're in a hotel room in the mid day of summer sun; white cotton sheets, and open windows without a breeze. He lays on his side covered to his waist; his scent intoxicating; wild and rough the texture of his skin, a new kind of velvet feeding my soul with his manliness, making me belong to him, again; all of me! Where is this coming from? I know! I'm being punished for saying I don't want to fall in love again; for denying love a future fall! I don't want to fall; I want to stay up and running, not necessarily in the opposite direction, but I don't want to crash with love, again!

(To get over a shock; to relive; to make sense; to take the blame; to overcome)

The closest to intimacy I got in months was a crowded bus! That kind of thing had never happened to me before, but guilty I am for knowing what went on! It wasn't a rainy day, so it wasn't somebody's umbrella. I didn't know what to do! Scream, get morally hysterical? What if I was wrong? I stood, all frozen up and tense; I didn't move an inch, but HE … he was moving his inches letting me know *exactly* where he was! I wanted to see what he looked like and tell him to stop it, but stupid me, I looked down! He was wearing a long topcoat. Clever idea; like curtains! He got off first; most men do! All frazzled and disoriented, I dropped my bags, missed my stop, I was a mess; furious and ashamed at myself for allowing this to happen!

(To assist; to reach out)

Weather permitting, I walk at night to clear my head and shed some calories. I enjoy people watching! It's safe to look at people; no one is looking back. Last night, I saw a blind man who lives in our building carrying a bag of groceries. He seemed confused and distressed, knocking his cane against storefronts as if he was having an anxiety attack. I crossed the street and approached him. I'll make you a deal, I said. We live in the same building, and if you pick up the pace, I'll get you there. He clutched my arm and off we went, steady and fast, the blind and the lonely. I asked if he was totally blind! It's all very blurry, he said! How blurry, I asked! Very-very blurry and dark, he told me! I crossed the line; I apologized and kept on walking. We got home; he took a moment and said, thank you! I can still hear it. That's how genuine it was!

(To tickle my fancy; to re-think; to re-examine; to regret)

I didn't want to need sex since my wife passed away, and at this age, it isn't much of a challenge not to! I think about it every now and then, but desire eludes me. I look at young people and I know they enjoy what's rightfully theirs. I beg your pardon! A pervert! You've got no poetry in you my friend! I sold the house, and bought a condo over there. Nice place; the hospital is four blocks away, and the cemetery only two! A group of us retired people meet once a month for tea in our party room. There's an older guy, older than me, in better shape, good posture, an interesting man whose father was from Greece; very proud of his heritage. A Greek! That should have clued me in, but at this age who thinks about those things! The tea gathering was over; he and I stayed to clean up. We did and sat to catch our breath. Made small talk, and don't know how, but he started to caress my thigh. What are you doing, I asked? "Aren't your thighs stiff," he said? Me too, I'm stiff; all that hair on your chest! I can't do this, I said, I have integrity! Look at the clock, he said, I'm eighty and you are seventy something, we don't have much time for integrity! Time! I used to be a Greek God, now I'm a Greek ruin ravished by the Turks, by earthquakes and lightning! Time is not on our side my friend, he said. And that was that! He didn't pursue it any further. Whatever his agenda was got me a little twisted!

(To overcome a shock; to lash out; to curse; to hold it together)

I need a moment. Give me a moment please, to understand how we have come to an end, you say? Why? 'Cause we're not as passionate and loud in each other's pants! Guess what? We're not twenty anymore! It's been 30 years since, look it up, mister! How old is she? Yes, she! Stop pretending you don't know what I'm talking about! Yes, she! How old is she? Don't! I don't want to know! I don't care how old, or young she is; I don't care about her; I care about what's going on now! Yes, now! Right this minute, ending thirty years of … what? What do I call them? Tell me what to call them! I'm going to need a moment here, a moment, to think!

(To count my blessings; to brag; to show-off; to reminisce; to entertain)

My first husband was perfect. I was in love! He was handsome and caring; a lawyer who advocated human rights all over the world. Fascinated by the good and the bad, he was fascinating to be around with. In the kitchen he was a chef, in the bedroom he was all man; the morning after, he was a room service attendant bringing me breakfast in bed in his white briefs. We were young and very into each other! He'd get his paper and read it at the chair across from me as I stared at him with admiration and respect. I loved everything about him. The more I had, the more I wanted! My desire of him never diminished. But, life's not fair, and ten years into our marriage, he had a massive heart attack. His heart was so full of love, it exploded! Needless to say, he broke mine! I still miss him!

My second husband, a doctor, was damaged goods, just a little! I missed my first, but my heart was big and had many rooms. I saved one for Herbert, and opened another for Joshua. We met at a political fundraiser and were instantly attracted to each other. I had been a widow for a year; I was young and needed a man's attention! Off to the bedroom, the altar, the bedroom, the bedroom, and that was that! Never got to another room! Didn't sit at the kitchen for a talk about nothing; we had nothing to talk about! It exhausted us and decided to annul the wedding for a reasonable settlement. Off he went, and so did I, for an extended trip to Europe. Europe! Europe is magical!

Spain was divine, and so was Pablo! There was a language barrier, but I didn't need language at the sight of a tall, dark handsome man with thick black hair dressed in loose white linen at his vineyards. I was in paradise with an angel pointing out the different varietals, and offering me grapes, which I swear had captured the sun and transformed it to nectar! His cellars were filled with oak barrels. The mysticism and magic of making wine was everywhere as he gently pushed me against the stone wall, and like a teenager in love for the first time I gave in! That was a vacation in heaven! I stayed for six months and married him. He promised to love, and I promised to obey. I learned everything I could about wine and Spanish literature in English! Life was good! It always is!

My third husband should have remained a part of the vacation in Spain. I was naïve and too infatuated to understand that you don't bring vacation goods back home, maybe a souvenir, but a husband? A vacation should stay a vacation and linger on in your memory. But, I didn't and after a great deal of paperwork, before family and friends, we exchanged our vows and started to spend a little time here, and a lot of time *over there*! I took up Spanish and though I didn't learn to dissect philosophical texts, I got by in a charming fashion! We had agreed to be equal partners, and spend time both here and *over there*! That was short lived! Equal partners with a good looking successful Spaniard, the only boy to a family with roots going back centuries! I just as well had been the ninth wife to a Sultan! Our cultural differences, in addition to the big pond drove us apart, and came to amicably agree that this didn't work. I did my best to create a win-win situation, but I'm not sure there is a win-win with any man you are divorcing. His ego got a little bruised and his way of showing it, or hiding it to be more exact, was to offer me a very handsome settlement! I often raise a glass of wine to his health and prosperity. He calls me on my birthday, as I do on his! After three husbands, I knew it was time to take a break, and I did!

I was six months into an official break from the sanctity of marriage. I had joined a gym, and went swimming religiously every morning including the Sabbath; I was never religious. I shared the pool with a gentleman in his sixties with movie star looks; well mannered, polite and a fast swimmer in his bulging swimming suit! After a few good mornings, he invited me to a healthy breakfast at a beautiful hotel nearby. Then it was lunch, then brunch, and many dinner dates followed by expensive champagne and imported chocolate! We were enjoying a second bottle of the finest bubbly when he admitted he was tired of being a widower, and how rejuvenated he felt in my company, and would I consider marriage! What was I supposed to answer to a 6.4" retired CEO with a doctorate in chemical engineering, topping me off with the body and stamina of a 25 year old? His understanding of the universe; his quest and desire to reveal its secrets of creation blinded me with brilliance; almost as much as the nine carat solitaire he proposed with! What was I to say? That I was taking a break? Six months was enough, and worth the wait for the five wonderful years we had together! His wealth accumulated like electrons to electricity! The autopsy showed he had a stroke and didn't drown while swimming. God must have watched over me—I hadn't joined him for a swim that day. I'd have been accused of foul play the way his children acted at the attorney's office over the estate with no prenuptial agreement! Paul was brilliant! Naturally, I gave him and our memories a big room in my heart, and my vault!

I wasn't planning on yet, another marriage. I hesitated in saying yes, but trusted an overwhelming sense of spirituality that struck me when I first laid eyes on John! I needed someone to need me, and this need for companionship ruled my life. My father died when I was six and though I wasn't consciously looking for a father figure, the safety of having a man to call my own sustained me. Living is good, but sharing life with someone is great! Growing individually while together is a contradiction I admit, but marriage wouldn't last a life-time if it was simple; if it didn't require a life's effort to master the ego and give way to a self-less acceptance of another! The lessons we taught and learned from each other were a match made in some metaphysical dimension. He embraced my doubts and subdued my fears in a consciousness of love. Two years later, he told me it was time for us to find others to teach and to learn from! I was the one with the resources. What he brought to the table was a free spirit and a well lived interpretation of life! I had my own tutor and didn't mind paying for it—I had plenty! I took the prenuptial to my lawyer who arranged for everything. I went home, opened a bottle of wine, looked at the tattoo each of us had gotten—a dragon fly; finished the bottle and rested; richer within and filled with wonder. I had learned that there are many answers to life's questions one can choose from, and each answer is right in that moment for the person who's doing the asking!

I made a career out of marriage. All of my marriages united aspects of me I didn't know existed. I can honestly say I have arrived at me! I am! I swore and promised God there would be no more ceremonies, but the occasional companion of a male friend. I stayed open and charmed, kept up with my social goings and doings, and threw myself to volunteer work at an animal shelter. That's where I became captive of true love and beauty in the eyes of the loveliest creature there is! A dog! I used to think that having a dog was some form of displacement and refusal to experience intimacy. I can hit myself for all the years I've cheated me from the purest form of affection! I have two beautiful girls; a Maltese Bichon I call Angel, and a Shi-Tsu I named Aasha; Arabic for life, or close to it! Like kids with different personalities compete for my attention. All they want to do is play! They remind me that life ought to be filled with play; that if I play with love in my heart, then living is exquisite and divine! They remind me to trust that I'm cared for and feel safe! Life is good!

(To regret; to speculate)

This gorgeous man approached me at the bus stop, and with a heavy accent said: "Hello, my name is Stan, I am from Poland!" He was too good looking and well put together to be a con, so I smiled! He said he was in the country for a month, that he was here to stay and wanted to make friends, soon! He asked for my number, to have coffee and practice English! Smooth! No one that good looking ever asked for my number, which I did not give him! No, I don't suffer from low self-esteem; I'm at peace with the mirror! I should have taken a chance. I could have asked about his life, his plans and dreams, even Poland! Was he a student? Did he come here to work? How? Does he have a permit? Am I, a citizen? There I go, jaded! This was my chance to teach English without going to Japan! What was I afraid of? Rejection! Like I was going to get into drug trafficking, or fall for him and call him big daddy if he thought he had a stable for me. I was just stupid, one more time, stupid!

(To cleanse; to rid; to dust)

I held on to your vicious letter for eight years. I didn't read it often, but its venomous content got under my skin and became my skin. Eight years! A letter—testament of hatred that crippled my spirit making me unworthy of all things good! The crow that nested in my heart paralyzed my ambition, and desire abandoned me allowing your cruelty to keep on punishing me. I gave you such power over me. I thought you knew me better than I could have known myself! I retreated in an exile of self-examination, and went on living without joy. I came across it yesterday and read it one last time. Guess what? It did nothing for me! It didn't affect, or influence this rebirth of spirit I've been experiencing! I took it by the lake, tore it up and threw it in the water. I watched your evil drown. I cleansed and baptized my heart anew! I am free of you, free from the darkness where nothing good can mirror itself!

(To connect; to wish it different)

Everything I did, I did for you father! I gave baseball a shot knowing I sucked, because I couldn't tell you I preferred swimming, synchronized swimming; it wasn't manly enough! So, baseball it was, and a practice or two at basketball, where without passion and affinity, my poor performance led to your disappointment. You were adamant on my participation in sports. It was the fee I had to pay for your approval and affection. Eventually, I grew up and learned not to expect it, though I needed and longed for it. It wasn't in you. You were caught up in a masculine version of a Rockwell illustration and affection wasn't one of its colors. Such were the times! Emotionally cheap and stingy, you cheated me out of us. You and me! I wish I could show you differently, but it's too late, it always is.

(To accept; to lash out; to prove)

Oh, my God! Oh, my God! Oh, my God! Thank you. Thank you the academy for recognizing me and my work! What an honor! I'm speechless. Thank you God! I want to thank all of the wonderful actors, the director, the producers, stylists, make-up, costume, lighting designers, the young man who brought me donuts and smoothies, everyone who surrounded me in this project! I can't believe it! Thank you. I want to thank my friends who supported and encouraged me every step of the way, and my enemies who pushed and infused me with determination through their hatred and jealousy, thank you! And you mother, thank you for telling me I will make nothing of my life. I will be sure to think of you when I sign my next five million dollar contract. Oh, my God! Thank you. A billion thanks!

(To justify; to extort; to manipulate)

Stop bribing me to go visit grandma! $20.00 meant something when I was fifteen! The car! I thought the car was for making the dean's list! I like grandma, but she has nothing nice to say! Last time, she told me that I look like a lesbian, and was I sure I'm not! She hates my jeans, my make-up; the way I sit, stand and speak. She went on to tell me that the problem with young people is that we don't understand, or care about poetry because we are in it, but we think we live in hell! Whatever! Ah, the poetry of youth with its vibrant and silky skin, she said! Don't leave out the acne, I added! She then went on about my earrings, my tattoo; the way I walk like a football player! What happened to women who lived to be women, she whispered! Do you know that she shops at "Forever 21?" I know she's rich, but you may not get to inherit as much as you think dad. She spends it all on top-of-the-line anti-blemish, anti-wrinkle, collagen everywhere! Give me another twenty.

(To welcome; to prepare; to gather strength; to overcome fear; to win)

AAhhh! I am excited. Aren't you? I'm not afraid. Yes, they'll tear me up; cut me open, so what? A woman's body is designed by God to bring life to life! So, here we are, hours away from being united in my life and dreams that support and include you, from here and beyond! I've been expecting you and I'm ready to love you, to inspire you; ready to teach you how to love me if you can! Blessed we are to be in America, part of its history in the making. America! Anything you want you can get, but right now there's nothing in this world I want more than you! Oh! I hope I'm enough for you, that son of a bitch your father; he took off; I couldn't make him stay, I've got pride you know; I didn't want him anymore when he accused me, that I intentionally became pregnant to keep him, tie him down; that son of a bitch accused you too, he said: "You and him, you're allies; this is a conspiracy; you women are brilliant at it, that's what my mother told me." Screw you and your mother; screw your mother, I said. So! I am going to be your father, too!

(To arm; to equip; to overcome; to compensate)

You've got to take it; ignore the ignorant, that's what I do; I try to be strong, to forget how they look at me when I clean their office, and sometimes I do forget that I'm a good and kind person, and I want to slap them for looking at me like what I do is demeaning! It bothers me, because it is derogatory to have another human being take somebody else's garbage! It hurts, because I'm proud to be Polish; and that's when I whisper Polish; polished, refined, better, smarter, funnier! And just because they work in an office doesn't make them better people; they lie all the time and pretend to like each other. Your father, that son of a bitch, he worked there too; he'd stay late; Oh, so tired, but not exhausted enough to flirt with me; all those sexual innuendoes and fantasies of sex on the desk; the executive and the cleaning lady! And stupid me, I let his fantasy become mine five nights a week on that desk. He was handsome, like you; that son of a bitch. Every time I clean that office, my blood pressure is on the verge of giving me a stroke. I don't want to, but after I clean, I spit. When I told him about you, he got a transfer overnight, God knows where; the son of a bitch!

(To apologize; to guide; to shed light)

You know this is the happiest you will ever be, 'cause you don't know that nobody promised you happiness, nobody owes you anything; this life is a fairy tale without a prince! This life is for dreamers! For those, who dare dream of the impossible; happiness! I still don't know why I kept you; it's insane! Times are crazy, the world is corrupt, the economy sucks; we are still trying to get on with the Republicans; we don't know if we're coming or going; what else do you want? Nothing's personal any more; personal is corporate, and if you are not corporate, forget it!

(To warn; to protect; to alarm)

There are people who want you because you are easy, or difficult, or a challenge! There are people who will do nothing unless they get everything; you body, your soul, your laughter; people who will bite your lip and make it bleed, so that you don't speak the truth any more; and touch your skin because they think that what they offer is what you ask, is what you need; what you cannot live without. There will be people who might care, or seem to care like cats alert preying for mice; these are the people you must keep your eyes open for and see; sleep not; rest not, they never do; they never sleep.

(To plan; to hope; to come to grips; to escape)

I can't avoid destiny; it manifests itself and finds me everywhere I go! I believe people mean what they say; I believe they love me when they say they do, in a state of orgasm! It lasts so little! I refuse to infiltrate love with doubt; to seek and not find; to long and not love, to grow and not bloom. I take nothing for granted; my only choice is that of a subconscious God; he who knows and dies when trust is forfeited by doubt. When I am ready, my destiny will take me to the place I am supposed to be! I will be ready to experience and choose with kindness all that I cannot avoid!

(To apologize; to explain)

I knew the moment you were conceived God entered my body, and my desire of you blossomed in a miracle of nature. You grabbed on to my insides and didn't let go. Having you in me was a roller coaster ride of emotions and hormones. You kicked often, in a hurry to come and see this world, impatient and impulsive I knew; I had a boy. You used and abused my body practicing a man's tradition, I endured. Giving birth was humiliating! Everybody was down there! Doctors, nurses, assistant nurses, assistant doctors! Eight hours in labor and endless pairs of hands probing my insides, you came and I forgot all pain. I didn't mean to hurt you when I said that I expect more of you! My insecurities have taken hold of me! I believe in you, I do! I believe there is a real opportunity for you to succeed instead of living your life day-to-day without direction. I wish great things for you. I promised to stay out of the way, to not taint your spirit, and love isn't an excuse for breaking a promise. Please, don't stay mad too long; I am your mother!

(To advise; to warn)

Don't do it like me! I passed up a lot of people who took an interest in me. I still don't know if I thought I was too good, or they weren't good enough! I gave myself no second impression, but the first. Instead of living the moment, I looked for the next! I should have thrown, immersed myself in every experience with intensity, instead of analyzing and dissecting to make sense of it. I was on the outside looking in, observing, not participating. I documented and measured life keeping me safe from living! I could have loved better, hurt more; had better sex; enjoyed all that was presented to me. I was a fool, good and stupid! Now settled and complacent, I am seasoned, experienced, a waste management of thought, a landfill of cancelled answers; exonerated grave sites! I'm not the happiest, but sadness is sweet in knowing that love came my way, but was too preoccupied with its definition!

(To narrate; to praise; to share)

Eros is a God, a ruler and a slave. He's devotion, faith, addiction. He's a wanderer, sadist, ventriloquist. He's bright; the eternal child of youth in the world and beyond. Eros is joy and sorrow, pain! He's the source and the destination, and we … we are his means of transportation.

(To pray; to hope; to invite; to call upon)

If you can hear my calling, if you can walk, won't you come near? Sense how my desire of you tortures my sleepless nights, and don't turn away the moment that something dear awakens in you. Obey the destiny that controls my desire to find and introduce you to all that we've lived; to encourage you to enter the same vision of a night's sleep in soothing colors of prayer and gratitude to us both, for recognizing each other behind the flesh, and finding the courage to rid our loneliness with each other's presence; presence alive, optimistic and sacred. Feel how sacred my desire of you is, and come. Please come, come and stay a while!

(To order; to inspire)

It won't kill you to become more sociable. Get out and meet the mystified people expressing their ideas, sharing their art, their passion for food, doing all they can to connect with you. Yes, you! It's immoral to be alive and not live! Quit acting like a hermit! Participating in social events isn't work. It is fun, and expectations are a part of it. Get out, meet and talk to people, you'll be surprised how self-inflicting your loneliness is! Go on without judgment and amaze yourself to find that this life-force includes you! Become the miracle people keep alive when doing something good. It's who we are! It's the sanctity of life!

(To find refuge; to retreat; to escape)

I take long walks by the lake and pray in an unusual way; I empty my mind and let me be totally blank. Black on black, white on white! It's all less important when I don't look for meaning. I enjoy walking in the fog at night. It's mesmerizing how it diffuses light, and hides the building tops that penetrate the sky. I like how it smoothes the sharp edges of life when clouds decide to visit. I can't see far, but I trust life revealing itself in my step. It includes me in a blessing of being alive, a part of this big secret of the universe drifting through my fingers embracing my spirit, and lifting me to touch the truth within me! It's only then that I'm at peace.

(To entertain; to move time forward and then hold it still)

Man the train was crowded! Someone in scheduling must have forgotten it was rush hour and this city of millions needed to get home! So much for the rate hike!

Thieves! All aboard, stacked too close for comfort, invading each other's personal space with bodies, hands, backpacks, hair in my face, cell phones, bad breath! Getting off was like re-positioning troops for battle! Stop after stop, the train got less crowded and showcased this absolutely gorgeous, well dressed dark blond man in his thirties, sitting with a briefcase on his lap! His hands, my God—big, strong hands, I wished I was an orange for him to squeeze. As his stop approached, he tried to get up, and I say tried because there was this big—big thing in the way—all proud and erect on the side, I gasped for air! I know he didn't get that by looking at me, so I looked around to see who provoked it! I was right! It wasn't me! It was a young, well not so young girl, twenty-eight if not more, good body, so-so face, wearing a short skirt sitting across from him with her legs crossed, the little tramp! He tried to cover himself with his jacket, lifted the briefcase up to no avail. I tell you, there was no hiding that!

(To entertain; to curse; to let go)

There was a time when I trusted desire, like I trusted your father! We were young and stupid, and in the sixties we idolized everything; even stupidity! It took years to realize it wasn't about love; love had nothing to do with it. We thought it did, and freed ourselves to having the raunchiest, best sex ever! I didn't love him. I loved that he was big, muscular, rough and twisted. I was inexperienced, but he taught me to enjoy pleasure without inhibitions and restraint. When I first saw him dressed in leather on a motorcycle, I thought I saw an angel. What I forgot is that Satan was an angel, too! But, we survived and turned out just fine, didn't we? I believed the odds were with us, and I was right!

(To accept; to entertain; to rekindle)

Instinctively, I knew you were different! I didn't want you to be like the macho son of a bitch father of yours, but … Gay! Well … that's not exactly what I had in mind for you; not because I mind gay, I embrace and support diversity as the true face of life! It's just that I would have liked you to offer your heart and father a child; to sow and reap the blessing of fathering yourself! Maybe he liked men, too! They say it might be genetic. You don't suppose I'm a lesbian?

(To reminisce; to bring it home)

I remember the day you came out like it was yesterday. I should have guessed when you went to see "Victor, Victoria" five times! We are everywhere, you said! The arts, politics, education, fashion, religion! Stop that, stop that right now. We are everywhere! We are all here, everywhere together. I wasn't shocked, maybe a little disappointed, I was right! Years later, I remember having a bourbon buzz, which prompted me to raise the question of what do, two men do? Don't tell me. I don't want to know! You didn't know what made you desire your own sex with such passion beyond reason. It just was! A hunger, a thirst to connect with your own, touch base, hit a home run worth a standing ovation! You said, it was like fireworks until they faded out, falling down from the sky. But, in those moments you were the fire and color in the works; you thought that God redefined, redistributed himself. A gay God if it was easier for me to understand! I'm not sure I do. It's not that important anymore!

(To entertain)

I'm no Puritan, but what's up with teenagers piercing and tattooing their bodies? Some are out of control! Is it some calling to mother earth? The sister moon! What? I got invited to a party! I went! There he was! An eighteen year old inked and pierced all over! Excuse me, I said, I'm older, have done my share of shall we say, unconventional things, nothing too severe; I'm not judgmental, or at least I try not to be, but I'm curious; what is it with the piercing, the tattooing and all this Gothic revival? He smiled and said; it just is! Brilliant! Is it a fashion statement, a sexual code, a shock value thing, a revolution, what? A little bit of everything, he said. Another brilliant answer! But, why so much of it! Is it you start with one and end up with a dozen? You can say that! Well, you know me! I ask the questions; I give the answers—the story of my life! How do your parents feel about it? They like it! I'm sure! A nose ring, pins and studs everywhere I could see, and I bet you beyond; like a Prince Albert—whoever this prince is, I'm sure he's not flattered to be a pierced penis, unless he was the first one to have it done! He also had a pierced tongue; he took it out and showed me a pin at least one inch long; I didn't know our tongue was so thick! And you can eat, talk and pronounce things right with that? The ring on your nose! What happens if you have the flu and want to blow? That little stud on the side of your nose, right there! I don't care if it's a diamond—it looks like a huge pimple even from up close! Is it true that the pin tongue, *tongue pin* makes for good sex? I had to ask! Oh yeah, oral sex is great with it. I didn't ask for whom! Doesn't it all hurt? Isn't all this self-inflicting pain some resentment for the body? How could he? He was so young! I wanted to tell him he didn't have to endure unnecessary pain; life is filled with it! But, I didn't! He was happy in the *just is* attitude, and besides, it wasn't my place to tell him! I'm glad I didn't!

(To let go; to abstain)

It's been a year, a year ago today since you left me so ruthlessly without a decent warning, an adequate farewell goodbye. You simply left, canceling out thirty years just like that! You were the hero of cowards to not tell me you had given up on everything; hope, too! I pray to God and tempt the devil for a chance to talk to you face to face, make you change your mind, implore you to include me in your time of need. I still don't know why you waited so long to tell me that your journey had come to an end! Spare me the pain. I wish you hadn't! Your dying devastated my desire to go on living. It's been a year, but, I promise not to cry. I'm not as fragile as I was back then, when I'd cry at three o'clock just because it was three o'clock, and I did! I'm stronger! I honestly am!

(To hold on)

I miss you being around on planet earth. It's funny how your quest to take off and liberate your soul, enslaved mine! It's unreasonable to expect myself to give up missing you. I'm on the verge of forgiving you, but can't bring myself to do it! Not forgiving you is my way of keeping you connected to me. Can't let go, but I do need to start loving somebody other than you; in addition to you! Someone, who's lived and survived the life terrific, and is fine with it; that someone, I want to love in an effortless kind of way with a restrained sense of excitement as we recall the times we experienced this and that emotion, daring to find a new angle to participate in it. Someone, who will electrify my body and alter the colors of my soul, reaching from the eternal past to the infinite future, all in one timeless moment! Is that too much to ask?

(To allow; to stand up; to disapprove; to seek justice)

My neighbor Gloria is stubborn and won't give up waiting for the Lord's Second Coming. At ninety plus, the Lord must visit her sometime soon. She will have her own Second Coming just like you at 25; me someday, and everybody born in and of this world—the child we love, the loving parent, the finest lover. Think about it! It makes me want to give up trying to live! But, it's real; like the Lord's visits; unannounced, sometimes unfair; his appointment book all screwed up! But, who am I to argue with the Lord? He hurt me; I'm right to argue, I stand up for myself, I'm not afraid of him; and if he was to come here, right now, I'd stare him in the eyes and ask him, why? I bet you, he wouldn't have an answer! You know why? Because God is all random, indiscriminate; it's fate, probability and chance!

(To follow advice; to try something new)

I got a new neighbor! Gloria, an odd old lady, who's up all night and gets the days all mixed up! The only thing she's got straight is the Rapture! If she tells me one more time that the Second Coming of the Lord is near, if not tonight, I think I'm going to messenger her over to Him. Stupid me, I told her I didn't believe in *salvation*. She quoted a third of the bible by memory with reference to chapters, and wouldn't stop like she was possessed. So, she's waiting for the Lord to come and *translate* her and her group, to that special place, right here on earth no less! Is it Hawaii, I asked! I've heard so much about the Second Coming, the other night I was in bed wondering, what if she's right! Right! There isn't enough science fiction for something like that happening! It's got to be symbolic! Pray. Try praying. It won't hurt you, she said, and I did! I prayed, not a sinner, but a person wanting to trade weakness for strength. I didn't tell her, but I've been praying to be true, authentic and noble in my battles!

(To imitate; to day dream)

My elderly neighbor asked me, if I believe in heaven and hell. Only in heaven, I said! Hell doesn't make any sense, it couldn't possibly exist and if it does, then it's probably right here on earth. We all go to heaven, right? I have been thinking of all the things I'd like to do when I go to heaven, she said. I'd like to lie on the grass and watch an anthill; walk at the bottom of the sea; witness the moment a caterpillar becomes a butterfly. I know I'm going to get a new set of choppers, and gobble up lots of corn-on-the-cob. Study all music, and play the piano with God in my audience. What a day it will be when we're completely transformed and one-hundred percent perfect! What a feast we'll have with all of my mother's home cooking, her very special rhubarb pie, and every desert you can think of! I think we'll eat for at least two weeks just to begin catching up. We all have a heaven to go to! Heaven is forever; it will take forever to do the things I didn't have time to get to! Have you thought what you'd like to do in heaven? No. Why? I try to do as much of it right here in hell, but there's one thing; sleep! But, you sleep a lot anyway. That's because when I do, I'm in heaven, and slightly depressed, is that okay?

(To chart a new course; to claim; to overcome)

I used to think I couldn't live without you in my life, but I do! I go on living, appreciating the most essential; you, in my life. Since you left me, I had to reconsider, and rethink it all; love it all allover again, and I'm getting to a place where happiness is peace! Thanks to you, I promised myself that I can do without *things* and people that don't add to my life, but clutter my happiness. I vowed to defect from this world game eating away my mind and heart, and substituting them with statistics on productivity. I can do without the fancy restaurants, the expensive furnishings, the private labels. Instead, I want time to feel; time to stop pretending I feel great. Time to be in charge; time to re-acquaint me without you in my life!

(To share; to reveal; to reflect; to praise)

To tell you the truth mister, I wasn't always crazy; at least I didn't think so! Homeless! Not something I planned! It all kind of got to me when life came crumbling down and pushed me over the edge! Every ounce of reason I had left in me, evaporated like the bitter cold wind that touches the water of this lake, and makes it steam, so it can freeze it. It's all too complex; maybe even trivial by now, like most things lose significance after a while; all things but love! Yes siree Bob, love stays and sustains; feeds, warms and inspires; and if the price for it is homelessness, then so be it! I'd choose it again a million times to feel it brand new, limitless, restless; comforting in it I am! You know, I thought I knew what love was, but you're a smart man, you know I didn't! I only thought I did!

I had been out on the streets for three years; kept to myself, until I realized that in order to survive the street and its ruthlessness, you've got to enter this competition of amazing craze; and if you can't win, you better be a runner up, or you're lost for real! You've got to compete with those who share the same destiny, and the ones who stretch the world so crazy from nine to five! I had been out competing, fighting and practicing straight jacket craze worth five Academy Awards, when I met Peter. Peter, the Greek! A once successful immigrant to the States for fifty some odd years! He impressed me with his stature, took me back with his walk; mesmerized me with the charming quality of his craze, and the awesome sanity in his eyes. I knew the moment he first looked at me, deep within my being that I was loved, and my heart opened wide returning this love, and I knew; I didn't think I knew, but I did; and guess what Mister; everything, every thing had found its place; I had found a home.

Peter and I, stayed together for a long time; moments short of eternity! We kept to ourselves and went everywhere together. People stared at us. We didn't beg, weren't dirty; they stared because we were different. Blessed is being different, you know! Do you? He taught me things I never thought to learn! To wear my coat even in the hot summer months; to save some heat for when it gets bitter and cold, and reflect on it. Our bodies will remember and tap into this heat when we need it, and we're surely gonna need it in this city! He was right! Wearing winter clothes in the summer was not a costume of craze; it was a necessity! He was the reason I survived it all, and to this day, I survive through our love, which was born to actualize the universe through us. That's how deep, profound, magnificent it was! It is!

I don't care if it's Sunday, or Thursday, which by the way is irrelevant on the street! I don't count time anymore; it's not like I've got appointments, or something. I look at the sun and tell time; the trees and flowers clue me in as to what month it is! Crazy, uh! It was a beautiful night close to Easter. The day was tiring with nowhere to stand still and rest! We were like birds wanting to stay on a branch a while, but a recurring shout kept us airborne! On the move and alert on the crazy stage, that day was unusually overwhelming; the energy was crazy! We found a quiet spot to rest the day at night; looked in each other's eyes and let go to rest. We kissed gently as I lay by his side, his arms around me. Suddenly, his weight became a little over bearing, and instantly I knew something was wrong, and it was; the whole god damn world was wrong; he had left me, he was gone!

I stayed a while; held him close I almost suffocated. I wished one last time in a lifetime of wishes, that this one wish come true; that every cell visible or not, remember and recall his presence; that every ounce of his spirit inhabit my being; and this one last wish, God was good, and it was granted; I felt it you know! But, you don't know! I can see you don't, and it's alright, we are different! Minutes before dawn, I pulled my crazy self together, ten times crazier and walked away. Didn't look back; I knew I had left not a thing behind. I wouldn't have been able to deal with questions from the police, or the coroner about how he died, and who he was! He was the essence to my life! What are you looking at? Crazy! I'll show you crazy. Oust!

(To reminisce; to make sense; to relive)

Oh, no! No man has been *down* there, if that's what you're asking! Assume nothing! Hard to believe an old gal like me didn't let a single visitor stay long enough to mine my precious goods! I was stubborn; equipped by guilt and high standards, discipline came easy! But, I've had my share of temptation to contend with! I tried to consent to the deed and I can prove it! There's not just one size, am I right? There was a man, I almost let have his way; strong and persuasive like a politician, Charlie! It was after a night's good music at this quaint jazz club on the South side, and one glass of wine that went straight through my head, that I came this *close* to giving it up! I let him rub against me, but I resisted him with an equal force of want and desire, denying him access! Since, I said no to someone like Charlie, I gave myself no choice but to keep on saying no!

What a man! Charlie, the dream man! Six feet two, wearing his shirt open to his navel when nobody dare do that! An artist he made something out of nothing; he talked anybody into anything he wanted, he was exhilarating—everybody loved Charlie, Charlie the artist; the biggest con-artist there was! He was unique, and so were my five years with him. One day he'd have millions, the next nothing; he was worth living for! His presence commanded so much attention. My God the girls fell over their counters, when he came to pick me up from the department store I worked at! I was in cosmetics! We were just friends; I couldn't be his lover; he wasn't the kind of man to stick around. I pointed to one of the girls who melted for him, and you know what he said? Her! I took her out, she's so absolutely normal, she bored me to death! That was Charlie! I looked forward to every new day; I was up to here with excitement, living in the fast lane! One night, we were driving around and I asked him to stop. I got out of the car and walked out on him; I couldn't take it anymore. That was the last time I saw him. Don't know what happened to him! I'm sure he did well! He was destined for greatness. I didn't know I was in love with him! I spent years hoping to feel that way again; if not with the same intensity, at least with the same disarming quality that falling in love has, to dictate all it wants making a complete fool out of you. But, miracles do happen; only in a lifetime!

(To take pride; to hold onto conviction; to justify)

It's a shame I stayed a virgin; dirty damn shame! Shame and guilt competed with my desire exceeding my human potential, but not my will! I was too embarrassed at myself, so I quit confession, but didn't stop praying and fasting trying to understand my body's aversion to sex! I became obsessed with what the virgin birth might mean! One night, after fasting for forty days, the Holy Mother appeared and sat right across from me, right there! She was splendid; dressed in a long wool brown dress, her face radiated light; perfect features! She embraced me with her Mona Lisa smile, and I felt the ultimate peace travel through me! It was crystal clear in that moment, that the purpose to discipline was to give birth to the purest part of me. It's been a challenge alright; ongoing and turbulent, but rewarding nevertheless; like betting against yourself and winning! Isn't that strange?

(To relate; to conceit; to spark a fire; to jump start)

I wasn't surprised when he took his life! I had watched him go deep to an abyss of emotional disorder. He'd crack a smile at a stupid joke, or two; a smile reassuring himself that what he was thinking and feeling was right! When I heard the news, I remember feeling numb and devoid of any thought; just like him! The signs were there. It was inevitable! We are not a feeling world, he said, we don't hurt; are not moved by tragedy; we are protected and immune to tenderness. Nothing changes except for the sky, but it tells me nothing when it does! I don't blame him for ending a life without hope and meaning! I too, can't recall the last time I was vulnerable and open to a thought, I could call tender! I've grown accustomed to neutrality; I have accepted the stranger sitting at my kitchen table in the morning having coffee and smoking a cigarette!

(To pray; to articulate; to dive within; to explore)

Sometimes, the unbearable pain of the world enters my heart, and with it the unfulfilled desires of children that come to play. Their dreams stay and linger on, taking over. Sometimes, I think I'd like to sacrifice myself for humanity and die a death like Jesus. If only, I could find a noble mission to immerse myself, and make a difference of that magnitude! No one can save us! If dying a death of sacrifice took the pain and suffering to the underworld, and kept them there forever; would I be willing? When does it end? Ah! The gift of death is salvation; it is the Second Coming! Sometimes, the desire to be happy for all overwhelms me into believing that I can do it, but I'm not strong enough! All I long for tonight, is to sleep in the arms of Jesus, and wake up rested; assured that everything will be better!

(To punish; to scar; to ruin; to tear apart)

I saw that! I saw how you looked at that boy! It was downright filthy and offensive. What's the matter with you, looking at boys like girls look at boys? Boys don't look at other boys like that? There you go again! There's something sick, perverse; unnatural about you. What's going through your mind only the Devil knows, and you surely are the Devil's child undressing other boys with your eyes! What are you so fixated about? What do they do when they see you looking at their crotch? They check to see if their zipper is undone! They're God's children!

God is there to protect them from your evil, self-indulgent and illicit desires! If curiosity, ever brings them your way; it doesn't mean that they like you! Everybody wants to see a freak show! Don't look at me like that! I know you understand!

(To arouse; to miss; to claim; to want; to long)

Every time he walked out of the door, I felt complete and clean, as if I had filtered all of my desires through him; receiving my purest being back through traces of, I swear love at the moment; it was, it must have been! He didn't have to touch me or kiss me, he was aroused anticipating; I liked that he liked me! I couldn't get enough of him; we had to take breaks; there was nowhere higher we could go, but climax; and it was all so right to end it. So, we'd continue where we left off; passion driving us to places divine. Oh, God! Oh, God, he'd drown a whisper; and I, like a slaughtered animal hid my pleasure in the presence of God, and silenced it in peace; a landscape of death; inviting, alluring, unavoidable! That's how we rested; life drying up in remnants of pleasure.

(To mislead; to misguide; to reveal a secret; to stretch a truth, or a lie; to show and lead the way)

I often enter his sleep; the big screen under his eyes I borrow; and I become all of Hollywood; and I give, every single Academy Award to … me! I appease him, entertain and seduce his fears to come out and play; I choreograph to dance with them, and I dance, dance, and dance all night long! All the visions that children see, like trolls coming down the chimney; my script! Chucky! My masterpiece! It was another boy just like him, longing to find that which he thought existed—a soul mate! Ha! Run, run in your sleep boy, run to find him, he's just turned the corner of a side street, a street that in my productions becomes the Auto Bahn! Maybe he'll be there, waiting to say hi, look you in the eye, deceive you into believing that HE, might be the one! Sometimes, when I'm in a good mood, I do wait at the corner of a picturesque, romantic side street; I transform myself to a lover, I lean forward, kiss him and press me against his thigh; I take his hand, put it inside my pocket and make him feel me. Sometimes, I am compassionate, I honestly am!

(To ban commitment; to relive pleasure; to attack; to stay true to conviction)

He was always a good time; put out in ten minutes notice. Something, everything about him made me want him! He'd cross my mind; I'd pick up the phone and dial fun! The man was born to please. I told him, if ever I had to pay for intimate service, I'd want the one providing it to be just like him—touching, fiercely connecting with passion, he worshipped me! I felt his body in one hundred spots, like needles sewing us together. I do please you, tell me that I do, he asked! He did! He was a natural who couldn't get and give enough; had the stamina of a warrior. Sometimes, he'd kiss me and breathe out all air from my lungs, and keep it inside him until he gasped for air. He loved to do it all, and I loved him for making me feel … beautiful! One night, he had just been pleased, and so had I when he turned his head away; I reached and grabbed his face, tears in his eyes. I love you, he whispered! Say no more! Get up, get dressed, and get out … not why, not because, go, leave, goodbye. Get out! I stood by the window and watched him disappear in the night; punishing him for thinking that love and sex have anything in common!

(To ask God to come clean; to give in to doubt; to strip the power of God; to make God real; to define God as human; to denounce God)

I'm afraid to call out your name 'cause I just don't know if you exist. But, if you did, would you help and guide me though I had the audacity to be in your own likeness and resemble your image? They say that you are kind, loving, forgiving. I'm so in need of kindness and love; affection yes, but not forgiveness. What have I done to seek forgiveness? Is having lived a sin? If you exist beyond my fantasy of goodness, beyond my dreams of justice, reveal yourself and speak in sounds more familiar. Touch and help me relate with a mind that tries to understand your cause and reason. I'm trying to come close to you; close to your conviction, but I can't! You don't exist! If you existed, you'd be my partner approving and supporting every choice of life and death I made to resurrect my soul while getting to know my body. If you were the God you claim to be, you'd play no games, no tricks, nor would you silence, when I need to hear you say that it's okay for me to feel that you have failed; that everything is not alright. If I have failed you, I've done so in your likeness and image, though you might have failed yourself for being absent-minded when you created me; empty hearted when you invested in my path of crossing the oceans, dreams as unattainable as you would be, if you existed!

(To eulogize; to pay respects; to cope)

I don't care about dying he said, so long as I can grow; and dying is an alternative way of growing, 'cause look at us the living, are we growing, he asked? I plan to grow you know; I never had a choice; and look at all the little deaths I have survived every time a little piece of the old me was won; forced by growth to dismantle itself leaving me cleaner. Little deaths are little miracles, he said, and it started to rain. I talk to my dead; they can feel and listen; they live through me; they are my home. Talking to them is the most reasonable insane thing to do. There's something powerful the dead can do—unite us; and we are one; until we forget them.

(To let go; to cope; to cut the ties; to say goodbye)

I did as you wished! You couldn't bear the thought of being buried in the darkness of the earth; you've had enough of it in your life! I baptized you through fire to cleanse and purify your body. Cremation is the noble, civil thing to do; I agree. It was windy and cold the afternoon I scattered your ashes. I opened the box that contained all six feet of you; the wind took over and off you went, just like you asked. You wanted to not be afraid to die; you longed for a mission in life, and hoped to find a purpose in death; and when you found one, you'd watch over those who aimlessly wander in the dark corners of the city. Look out, you said, you never know whose crazy mouth I might borrow to speak to you, whose insane mind I might inhabit to tell you where I've been!

(To release; to let go; to let the pressure escape)

It's been a year, a year ago tonight since you left me. It was so unfair. It still is! Give it a year you said, time would heal, make me forget; well ... it hasn't. Can't get you out of my system! I have planted you inside me like a tree; protect you with the walls of my heart, and I feel good, but then I recall you leaving me stranded; and I want to uproot you, throw you out, let the snow burn you, be done with you. I had prepared for you to leave; had made myself hear your last goodbye every time I went to bed, waking up without you there greeting me good morning; damn it, I had prepared myself, I had ... and when the phone rang; I knew it was a matter of days; I hesitated in answering. God! I thought I was ready to take it! I remember time standing still; getting down on my knees, losing it ... I couldn't cry. Oddly, I picked the bible; opened it and read the first thing my eyes fell on to: "All transgressions are forgiven." That's when I knew that you went to heaven, and the funny thing is that's where I'm going, too! Save me a spot, so we can be together!

(To present the findings; to regret having been nice; to acknowledge one's stupidity)

Many boys were attracted to me! I was cursed with beauty. I went to bed beautiful; I woke up more beautiful! I was never unkind to men's advances and admiration. I met up for a drink with almost everyone who asked me! I thought this charitable act of kindness was enough, but it led them to believe I was interested in the bedding department! Two or three dinner dates later, and after having been honest and personally non-personal, this beauty queen was dumped and left feeling stupid for having been gracious to avoid hurting their feelings! Now, that hurt me! To get dumped by someone less good looking than you, poorer, less educated, older! That hurts! Honey, you're not qualified to dump me! Become an executive, a CEO, go and learn how to speak properly, and I'll be happy to tell you what I really think of you!

(To come to terms with the past; to give one's self credit; to gamble and win; to give thanks)

My parents' wedding gift to me for eloping with a gentile man who I married, was disinheritance! In our household being Jewish was the first priority, a doctor second, a male third, and a woman fourth, if that! I did manage, but when life got rough, I missed the B.D., before disinheritance days! Before disinheritance, all I worried about was if the maids would show up for work after their day off; and how old I'd be before I had my own driver! My parents had money, lots of money, but death came not discriminating paying my family his respects. My mother dies at forty, and with her all of the advice she was supposed to give me along the way; my father at forty-two not having redone his will; my grandparents shortly thereafter; all from cancer. In my family, we didn't need Hitler, we had cancer! No one was affectionate, nor were the servants—they were not paid to kiss hello, and hug goodbye! So, when I met my husband, I sacrificed it all for his endless affection and care, and it was all worth it!

(To present; to connive; to plot; to scheme; to conspire; to get carried away)

You are boring him to death, dear! If you keep this up, he will leave you for another woman, who is fun to be with! Keeping a man around isn't easy, especially one who's as cute and desirable as your guy! Stop thinking about menial problems and focus your attention on how to keep him, before he leaves you for another! Then, it will be too late! Wake up to the fact that you have a man around and do something! Cook for him, but not in the traditional time; cook for him at two in the morning; tell him you read that the body's metabolism to vitamins is best at two in the morning! Feed him and get him drunk; pretend that you are drinking, but don't! Change the boring pajamas to sexy lingerie, because it is … too hot in the house! Take the armchair next to the couch he's sitting at; get up often, so you can sit back down often to touch your thighs, caress your breasts; to tilt your head back, and do all you can to seduce his *desire!* Before you know it, he'll ask you to go and sit next to him. Don't! He actually wants to come to you himself. Show him that it's easy, invite him with your silence; think about it intensely in your mind; say nothing! He'll read your thoughts! So, now he's on his knees trying to get your intimate attention, but this one night you mustn't give in! Oh, he will try; he will caress the back of your neck; he knows that it excites you! Take his hand with power; yes, physical power; hurt him a little; look at him intensely; tell him without words that you love that, and move his hand to your breasts. Let him enjoy some, but remember that you mustn't give in; not tonight! Create a memory of seduction; make him desire you all day the next day at work; make him lose his job because he's thinking of you! Seduce him to the point of no return and make him stay; you've given him no other choice!

(To tell it like it is; to unmask; to attack)

It's raining, but it hasn't been bad! We haven't seen winter yet, and it's March already! Isn't that nice? It's nice in New York; all the intellectuals come to New York. Intellectuals! Brooklyn Bridge! Oh, it's only 14th Street! I'm an intellectual. I don't like the train; I prefer to ride by limo if the price is right! I lived in the ghetto; forty years, I lived in the ghetto, all the intellectuals live in the ghetto; it got dangerous; I moved! Woodside, Queens, where all the Cinderella wives live with their expensive cars and the expensive husbands. It's boring and I miss the ghetto, but I visit often, I still have friends there, my intellectual friends. I am an intellectual! Brooklyn Bridge! Let me see! I don't take this train. I take the 4, the 5, the 6, the N, or the R; I like them better! Why did I take this train, I hate it! We come to America! We come to America to learn English! Everyone in Puerto Rico wants to come to America! "We are America," my father said. But, we come to America and when we get here, we say, America! America! America! Is this Brooklyn Bridge? Brooklyn Bridge, City Hall, Chambers! Does anyone know? Where is Brooklyn Bridge?

(To report; to delegate; to assemble; to campaign; to stir)

Thank God I'm back, safe and sound, from a city where safety is not a precaution, but a standard of living in itself! Nothing affects or sways Pittsburgh; it is dedicated to boredom and beyond! Pittsburgh! I felt like I was in heaven; Satan in heaven! Scary, isn't it? Impossible, you say? It's true in Pittsburgh! I'm sure the cross is happy to have won over my inability to tempt anyone, not even on Saint Patrick's Day to an immoral thought, let alone a wicked action! For a moment there, I thought an insurance salesman harbored an extramarital desire for me; wising up later it was naïve curiosity over my bright, sparkling new dress! I was blinded with frustration! It drove me crazy to see all races getting along and coexisting peacefully! I felt like I needed counseling! But, who's there to counsel Satan; God! We've got to do something about it! Move my headquarters to Pittsburgh; announce a competition amongst my staff that whoever wins the most followers gets a promotion, bonuses and time off to enjoy the spectacle of our newcomers despair and grief! Yeah! That's good! Shut down some industries; people will be out of work, owe money, start drinking and get physical, abusive, in and out of jail! Oh, yeah! That's great! A complete breakdown in communication; no one happy with their spouse, everyone running after strangers for some understanding, committing adultery, hoping to find what they had before; hell, what they have now! We've got to do something about it before I'm totally disgraced! What are you looking at? I'm gonna shake 'em up a little!

(To hold on; to blame; to torture)

I could've had any team captain in high school. My double D generals commanded attention and desire! Instead, I married a softy one! Polite, caring and good around the house, I should have known that straight men, who plan on staying straight don't learn to bake pies, and certainly don't like Streisand, Marilyn, Betty Davis, Judy and Lisa! It took me a year to come face-to-face after he proclaimed his love for another man! You look good, he said. Thank you! Are you seeing anyone, he asked? Four kids, a job, and a house to keep up, I don't think I have the time to meet anyone! You! How are you, and him! Oh, please, quit playing the victim, go light on the Catholic guilt, he said! Forgive me! For all it's worth, he said, you were the only woman I was ever attracted to! Thanks! So, how are you guys getting along? You've moved in together! Bought a penthouse on the 52nd floor, and a dog! You look happy! I am, he said! Good, 'cause there's a hell somewhere over the rainbow you know, enjoy it while it lasts! Eventually, I will accept him, it, them; I have no choice, but he doesn't need to know that!

(To endure; to surpass; to overcome)

Back home in Mexico, we had it all; great weather, fresh fruit, sugar cane, everything; except for one thing; premarital sex! We were more catholic than the pope; never talked about sex in our home; a vague and rare reference to it was plenty. When I had to run an errand, my mother spit on the street and told me to be back before it dried! You do the nasty thing *mija*, no man will be your husband. Good girls don't look at boys; they look down; not their crotch, down at the tips of *your* shoes! I obeyed and stayed a virgin all excited and hungry for the first night with my husband; now, the ex! All my expectations and fantasies about the greatness of sex went down the sewer. It was lousy! We were off to a bad start and didn't get any better. No fore play, no passion; the same position, same endurance, me, me, me! Him, him, him! *Cabron*! I got pregnant back-to-back; three children in five years, so I wouldn't have sex with him! Six years into my marriage, my parents died in a bus accident when a couple of chickens got loose inside the bus, and the driver drove it off of a cliff! How Mexican is that! Their death was my liberation. I divorced his ass, took my children and moved to America to live with my aunt, and I've never been happier!

(To inspire; to guide; to reward)

I've explored every idea, and the idea that followed, and the one after that. You kick the ball and kick it again until someone kicks it back to you. Not every idea works out, but there's no fun if you don't play ball with life! You keep kicking until arthritis gets in the way to slow you down; until your vision gets blurry and can't see where to kick it, and to whom! Yes, you burn out. Take a break, but know that the will to plan a dream comes up again, and gives you the energy and the resources to transform the idea into action from the intangible to the real of now! You've got to make life pay you back! Demand a return of the investment in you. You owe it to your spirit. Kick the ball, improve your plan of action, and kick the ball again. This is the game plan of life, the intelligence behind desire; the marketing of life. If you can think it, create it and make it real. Give yourself no other option.

CHOOSING A MONOLOGUE

In an audition, the person—actor is the character. It is unreasonable to expect any actor to develop and convey a full fledged character with just one monologue in an audition. What is doable though is that the actor can incorporate strong character elements, and make acting choices to bring the monologue to life in performance.

You and the monologue you choose are your business card; how you present and represent each other should inspire those that you are auditioning for to do business with you!

When a monologue grabs you, make sure it feeds you to make acting choices you can carry out! Often times, actions and physical activities that you should use will arise from spending a few days with a monologue. Memorizing should be the last step. If you are unsure, ask a colleague if a monologue is right for you! A friend's objective perception of you reading a monologue is a good start. In other words, you and the monologue must have a compatible physical and spiritual connection to produce a credible match in an audition.

It is also perfectly acceptable to choose against type. An actor doesn't have to be young and voluptuous to act the part of an exotic dancer; or in great physical shape to be a personal trainer at a sports facility!

Type casting is stereotyping without the negative and moral clichés attached to it. In a very competitive and abundant pool of actors, casting an actor who looks the part is a smart and cost effective way to produce any artistic and commercial project, if the producers and directors are looking for the obvious.

It's worth spending sometime type-casting yourself. It may be difficult, but worth the effort as it can help you create a marketing strategy to follow, and go after parts that are suitable for you. The more types you cast yourself in, the broader your market becomes as you go about the business of acting; its art and the money. Make it happen by knowing and pursuing your market, and rightfully get your market-share!

Choose a monologue that showcases your acting style and suits your personality. Use this artistic equation to get cast.

HEADSHOTS

You are called in as a result of your headshot and are expected to live up to the perception the caller has made of you based on that headshot. The photographs that you are using should be as close to the real you as possible. A great image of you, if it isn't one that you can duplicate and bring to an audition or a casting office, is not going to work!

Many actors' headshots clustered together look alike because actors choose image and glamour over who they really are! Express your individuality and don't mask, or disguise it. Be honest and truthful about *who you are* right now in your life and career; it is what makes you unique, different and truthful! Respect the process and find the joy in it, which will take you to the next step.

An effective commercial option to a headshot is a double-sided black and white composite card like the ones models use, with a close-up of your upper body, and a couple more photographs that include character elements of parts you are suited for. What parts do twenty year olds get? College oriented films, or big brother-big sister family parts in general. Instead of looking like an aspiring movie-star, why not look like a big brother, or a college student; a swimmer if you can swim; a teacher, or a coach! If you are athletic, consider a photo in gym gear at a sports field, or health club. Wardrobe, make-up, props and location are tools to get you cast by suggesting to those who are doing the casting that you are right for a part.

PREPARING A MONOLOGUE

Treat creative text like music and find its rhythm. Rhythm in music is the beat. The beat can be even or uneven; steady or unsteady. Each monologue has its own rhythm. In addition to the rhythm, there is tempo. In music tempo is the speed of the music. Nail down the rhythm of the monologue you are preparing and work on the tempo, which must change often to make your performance interesting and effective. Monotone is artistic suicide. Rhythm and tempo with the right amount or projecting, articulating and enunciating are a must have—must do!

If the rhythm in the monologue you would like to perform isn't clear to you, and after you've given it your best shot; write the monologue down without any punctuation; then go back and add your own punctuation. It's an interesting way of discovering, or inventing a new rhythm in a monologue.

Prepare your monologue by deciding the *where*, *who* and *why*, which is the action. Incorporate physical activities to the three elements above and you have a real chance of getting cast.

WHERE ~ Find and decide on a place where this monologue could happen. Is it a kitchen, a living room, a therapist's office, a church, or a restaurant! Is the restaurant quiet, or congested with a lot of people sitting close to you. Put your character in a place that stimulates and adds to the performance. If you were the devil; a church would be the most interesting place.

WHO ~ Make a choice as to whom you are addressing the monologue to! Is it your mother, a best friend, a husband, a lover, a school teacher, or a priest! If you were at a therapist's office; is this your first time? If it's the first time, your body may show some discomfort if your action is to reluctantly confide; or your body would be at ease if your action is to seek help! How you feel about whom you are addressing will determine your physicality and tempo.

ACTION ~ An action is the why and the actor is the how! A very good overall action for any audition is to 'get something off you chest.' Go in with this mindset; the rest will fall into place and you'll do very well. To defend, to convict, to castrate, to defy, to relive, to condemn, to accuse, to lash out, to blame, to protest, to beg, to implore, to excuse, to appeal, to protect, to let go, to dismiss, to forgive, to implore; are all actions which have an inherent physicality. If you have chosen to implore as an action; your character may implore on his knees; or across the dinner table. You would need to decide how the character goes about imploring, whom and why! We implore parents differently than lovers; if a parent is about to disinherit you, and inheritance if of value, the way you'd implore that parent can be extraordinary since the stakes are high. If your action is to dismiss; how you feel about who you are dismissing will determine the measure and lengths you will go through to carry out the act of dismissal. We dismiss children differently than we do adults. If the person that you are dismissing may never come back as a result of your action, and you care for that person; then the stakes behind your action of dismissal are high!

There can also be action phrases such as: To cast a spell on you; to swim my way into you; to make you see it my way; to destroy your memories; to ruin the happiest day of your life! Choose an action, spend some time understanding it and try it out physically.

Often the action comes naturally in rehearsing a monologue, and finds its way out of you based on who you are, what you look like, what's in your soul and how you interpret the material.

Tap into this knowledge when rehearsing your monologue and it will take you there. Don't be afraid to choose a villain action; show contempt; a bit of hate; disapproval! To avenge; to disregard; to ruin someone's day; to dismiss; are all powerful and very interesting actions to take on. Actions that present a neutral character are often too safe and potentially boring!

Our lives are filled with actions we carry out both consciously and subconsciously all of the time. Actions are the motive to getting things done; to getting our way; to getting others to do what we want them to! It is within human nature that we plan on winning in any action that we undertake; yet, we often lose, but not until we have given it our best shot at winning, and certainly not until the very end! This is why you should *play* to win. Acting and carrying out an action with high stakes and the determination to win, are elements of characters we enjoy both in real life and on stage!

In the beginning of each monologue I have included some potential actions that you may find helpful, and may guide you to your very own action.

PHYSICAL ACTIVITIES ~ Dress up the action with a physical activity. Put on eye glasses; take them off; play with a scarf; adjust your clothing; do your nails! Personally, I like when characters have behavioral tics such as blinking, stretching one's neck back and forth, clearing one's throat, an intermittent lift of one shoulder! Start your monologue with an obsessive and repetitive behavioral pattern, and use as often as you like, or deem necessary. If you know magic tricks, make them a part of your character. Incorporate an accent if you can sustain it. Character elements give you ownership and make your audition performance special and memorable.

The beautiful thing about monologues is that fifty actors can perform the same monologue and each performance will be different. The richer the presentation, the more interesting the performance; the better one's option of getting cast! Exercise that option!

GETTING A CALL TO AUDITION

When someone calls you to schedule an audition, good telephone manners are essential. In this day of voice mail and cell phones, responding almost immediately is a step closer to getting cast. Those who call to schedule an audition, take notes such as date and time they have called, and their impression of you. The logistics are the same as with any other job interview.

If the time you are asked to come in does not work for you; politely ask if another time is available. If you can change your plans, try and accommodate. Remember that there are dozens of others who are also being called in. If setting a time for you to audition becomes too much of a production; the easiest and most productive step for the caller is to pass you up!

Ask what is it that they would like to hear, so you can best prepare for the audition. Keep all ads you've responded to handy for quick reference; do some research if possible on the production or theatre company that's calling you in for an audition. The more you know about what kind of work they produce, the better you can prepare and feel at ease when you get to audition. It's also a good idea to get a telephone number to reach them should something unexpected come up.

Be on time; audition well; thank everyone and leave. You've done your part. This is no time for questions about the production, rehearsals, pay, etc. Any information you would need to know, would have been given to you. Anything more will be presented to you at a call back.

Do tell those who are casting that you are punctual, professional, easy-going, non-judgmental, a team player who is inventive with acting choices. No one wants to work with a know-it-all who has an opinion about everything. Unless you tell, no one will know, or find out that you are punctual, professional, easy-going, inventive and open to direction; eager at trying out and exploring different angles!

How you communicate, what you ask and how you sound over the phone predisposes the caller on whether you are an actor one wants to work with. Getting called in to audition is half the battle of landing a part. Good personal and artistic qualities measure well together.

AUDITIONING

Don't rush you monologue because you are nervous. Take a moment before you start and find the source of its truth, which forces you into action. Taking a private moment in public view is very interesting to watch. Keep in mind that this is the first time they are seeing and hearing what you are presenting.

If you are asked to do a cold reading, you will and should be given a couple of minutes with it. Then, give it a shot. If nothing else, decode the rhythm of the text. That is sufficient proof that you are an intelligent actor. If you are in tune and want to try two versions of the same cold reading, I don't think anyone would turn down your offer to do so. When in doubt go the opposite way the text leads you to. If the character in the text is serenading a lover; casting a spell is a far more interesting choice.

Make sure that you are heard. There are many actors who think they are heard, but aren't! If you are not heard in a small room, what would happen on stage? If you are not heard, and one isn't wearing a hearing device, your audition is over! Instead, take the room; and the one next to it; the entire building if you can. It's a lot easier to scale back an actor than assume that there is more volume and ability to project!

Most actors play it safe during an audition reserving choices with risk for a performance, which will not happen as a result of a safe and consequently boring audition. One thing! Move, move, move! Think of your character as a caged animal looking for a way out. It will do wonders for you. It will make you move about, feed you, energize and sustain your action. Moving is imperative. Any audition, which does not require you to be in the center, as in a television commercial audition, should in my opinion take place in any spot, except for the center! Standing and delivering a monologue center-stage is often amateurish and boring. Take the corner; start your monologue with your back, then turn; find a reason and the justification to look up; look down; look away and keep on moving; don't just stand there!

Even if you aren't right for the part, you would leave the audition a winner. Adding these touches to your audition will not leave you feeling that you could have done better; you would have given your best performance, and trust me when I say that you will be remembered, and being remembered keeps the door open for more calls. Industry people talk to each other; share the needs and demands of their projects, and recommend actors who have impressed them.

CREATING OPPORTUNITY

There is plenty of work for those who have a clear picture of what parts they are best suited for. Pay attention and respect the uniqueness of the person the actor originates from; that would be *you*! It is the honesty and truthfulness of you that produces confidence in your craft.

Acting opportunities exist in many more places than a Hollywood set. Look to your artist friends for collaboration and training. Try out cities close to where you live; sublet an apartment short term; explore acting opportunities; seminars and workshops; audition, audition; audition every chance you get. The more you audition, the better you become!

Let go of expectations and responsibility from your psyche in landing a part, any part, anywhere. Your mission is to prepare, show up and give it the best that's in you at that moment. Having a good time while performing is contagious to the decision making people doing the casting! First and foremost, make auditioning fun and exciting for you and don't leave this personal reward out of the process. Kick the ball and continue to kick it until someone kicks it back to you, and then you have a game!

EPILOGUE

If you have found this book of monologues inspiring and satisfying, please recommend it to your fellow actors, family and friends. I kicked the ball. Now is your turn! Enjoy!

Many thanks and best of luck,

Nick C. Koroyanis

978-0-595-46985-7
0-595-46985-X

CPSIA information can be obtained
at www.ICGtesting.com
Printed in the USA
LVOW08s1446230417
531876LV00001B/178/P